Room Of *Imaginary* Creatures

teshima

Preface 6
Half-eaten Lion - J. Whitney 11
Fish in a Bowl - J. Rossander 16
Ass - F. Pitt-Kethley 18
Train Guard - T. Bruzon 20
Wolf - N. Jones 22
Leopard - Yorùbá 24
Slug - J. Whitney 26
Golem - F. Pitt-Kethley 30
Money - J. Rossander 31
Ear/Window - N. Jones 34
Hyena Man - Yorùbá 36
Cormorant - F. Pitt-Kethley 38
Traffic Jam - J. Rossander 40
Horse - T. Bruzon 44
Fish - N. Jones 46
The Egúngún - T. Ipadeola 48
Tree - A. Perrino 50
Me - H. Willemyns 52
Antelope - Yorùbá 54
Sheep - J. Rossander 56
Louse - J. Whitney 59
The Writer - L. Diependaele 62

24H Starbucks - J. Rossander	64
Buffalo - Yorùbá	66
Brown Bear - J. Rossander	68
Perfect - J. Whitney	71
Oranges - C. Unigwe	74
Moon - A. Perrino	76
Snow Globe - J. Rossander	78
Dodo - F. Pitt-Kethley	80
Dead Man - T. Bruzon	82
All the vacant fields of China - J. Rossander	84
Mechanic - N. Jones	87
Spike - J. Whitney	90
Cloud/Puddle - J. Rossander	94
Dragon - F. Pitt-Kethley	97
Drill Monkey - Yorùbá	98
The Priest - T. Bruzon	100
Black Astronaut - J. Rossander	102
White Socks - C. Unigwe	104
Full Moon - Tsu Ye	108
Inuit - G. Hart	110
Exit - M. Ladd	112
Ten Years & Three Days - A. Qi	114
A Quiet Twin Bed - O. Verissimo	117

This collection of poems was written by musicians and poets as part of a project that researches the connection between music, poetry and prostitution.

It all began as I struggled to write a scenario for a film that would help me understand what it meant to be a musician. I had been a professional musician for almost 15 years and I had been a music-lover for almost all my life. I owed everything to music. But the world of music was changing dramatically. The structure was collapsing. This gave me my first idea: My movie would start with some ominous lines of poetry that I adapted from an ancient Yorùbá-hunter poem.

The music business is a scruffy animal
it devours the dreamer
together with the feathers
in which they are flying

That scruffy animal is dying.

Movie starts...
Good. We're off! A kick in the nuts of all those TV talent-shows that feast on young people who want to make it as a musician! A boot in the face of the old music factory turning hard talent into mush!
Right! And what happens next? What will happen if the Old World of Music disappears? If record-sales are finally ground to a halt?
If you have to compete with 1 billion bands that all use the same tools and channels?
Would musicians have to become prostitutes in order to survive? Would that be so wrong? There didn't seem to be that much of a difference between music and prostitution. Intimacy as currency.
In the old days, courtesans in Japan and China were well-versed in Music and Poetry...

So I set about contacting musicians and poets with a simple question: 'Can you write me a poem from a prostitute's point of view? Can you describe me a lover, a customer, a feeling?'
I hoped that their poems would provide me with insights and metaphors that I could use in my movie.
And they did.
And so I wrote and completed my first full feature film.
I called it 'Birdsong' and it told the story of a young woman in Tokyo who was dreaming of a music career but ended up a prostitute. The title referred to an ancient fable about a bird that had to stick her head down the dark throat of a lion that was choking on a bone.

But the poems were many and alive in a different realm so the idea of a book, a bestiary of sorts, slowly started to take shape. A book that would be an album at the same time, a place to capture songs, the register of a brothel...
The records of a *Room of Imaginary Creatures.*

I want to sincerely thank everyone who contributed to this exploration. I know some of you went to very dark places to get this on paper.

Hendrik Willemyns

Dedicated to Grant Hart
(1961 - 2017)

HALF-EATEN LION

Johnny Whitney

My visitor tonight
is a half-eaten lion
limping to my room
from the wreck of an old friend's bachelor party
drunk off his ass
hindquarters gnawed to the skeleton
from stripper sweat

I've seen his type before
ages ago in college
when I was younger
shouting conversations in each other's ears over searing house music
Jägermeister shots
Jägermeister shots
Jägermeister shots
It's 3 AM the club is closing
we stroll down drizzling Manchester streets
huddled together in the cold
nowhere to go
It's not depressing when you are in your early 20's
the homely smell of breath
listening for the first birds of the morning
then blackout
it's all very familiar

"please?"
He slurs
"Pretend you're a naughty nurse.
I'll be your patient?"

I blush
My tits turn to bags of battlefield amputation stumps
I dump them on the floor unceremoniously
then deliver a hasty morphine injection
to our foreheads
we fuck under a zombie sun
while tourniquets tighten
tighter
to try to beat back death another hour

"please?"
He slurs
"Pretend you're a sexy secretary
I'll be your boss?"

I unbutton my mouth
all
the
way
down
my boots give birth to 10,000 cups of watered down coffee
we schedule real meetings with fake plants
then
the pounding, punishing echo of typewriters overtakes us
we wrap our numb limbs around each other
like soldiers crouched in doomed trenches
our lips graze
fluorescent lights cackle overhead
and we cum like fountains in well lit coffins

"please?"
He slurs"
"Pretend you're the hot and bothered teacher
I'll be your student?"

My eyes liquify
A flock of rare beautiful birds erupt from the pools of smeared black mascara
curious
we track them
for miles and miles
then exhausted
we lose them in a clear cut forest
nothing but neutered tree stumps for miles
and oh
the unsheltered vastness is so fucking cold
we huddle together for warmth
and spend the rest of the night
describing sunlight
to an unending dial tone

A permed wig is lowered from the ceiling

"please?"
he slurs.
"dress up like a bride on her wedding night
I'll be the cockeyed best man
your man"

then he drifts
involuntarily
into a whiskey greased slumber
deaf dreams of dry planets
drifting

I slide open the balcony door
23 stories up
throw on a hotel robe
and lay out in a night sweetened deck chair

beach sounds fill the air
syncopated by the horde of restless skyscrapers
lurching toward the moon scarred sea

FISH IN A BOWL

Jenny Rossander

My visitor is a Fish in a Bowl

A staring contest
That was carefully placed here
By a couple of his friends
Half an hour ago

Taking up half of the floor too

I fondled the glass of his
Spheric home
For just a second until he
Instantly
In a shrill tone
Asked to just wait here with him
So his friends would think…

These 30 minutes
In his nervous breakdown
silent company

I should have charged extra

ASS

Fiona Pitt-Kethley

Hung like a donkey, but not much upstairs.
Only Titania, doped by Oberon
could tolerate his type for very long.

Once he is in the room the room feels filled.
Braying with pride, he cannot realise
his noisiness is not a welcome sound.
He opens his mouth, displays his wonky teeth,
pricks up his ears, standing beside my bed,
laughs for the sake of it, at anything.
Size is not everything. He thinks it is.

TRAIN GUARD

Timothy Bruzon

My visitor is a train guard
Always on time
Reliable as desire

He counts down dozing commuters
Their heads nodding
Like wild flowers in a Summer breeze

Every face tells him something
Every dark toned suit.
And part worn shoe

The thrill as each passenger
Reveals their hand
Players in his travelling card game

I role-play a lost fare
Late night giggling drunk
The last in an empty carriage

Open mouthed
And on my knees
I search for the lost ticket

His voice deep and steady
The monotonous drone
Of clacking wheels

Finally we sleep
Lying together
Like two warped tracks

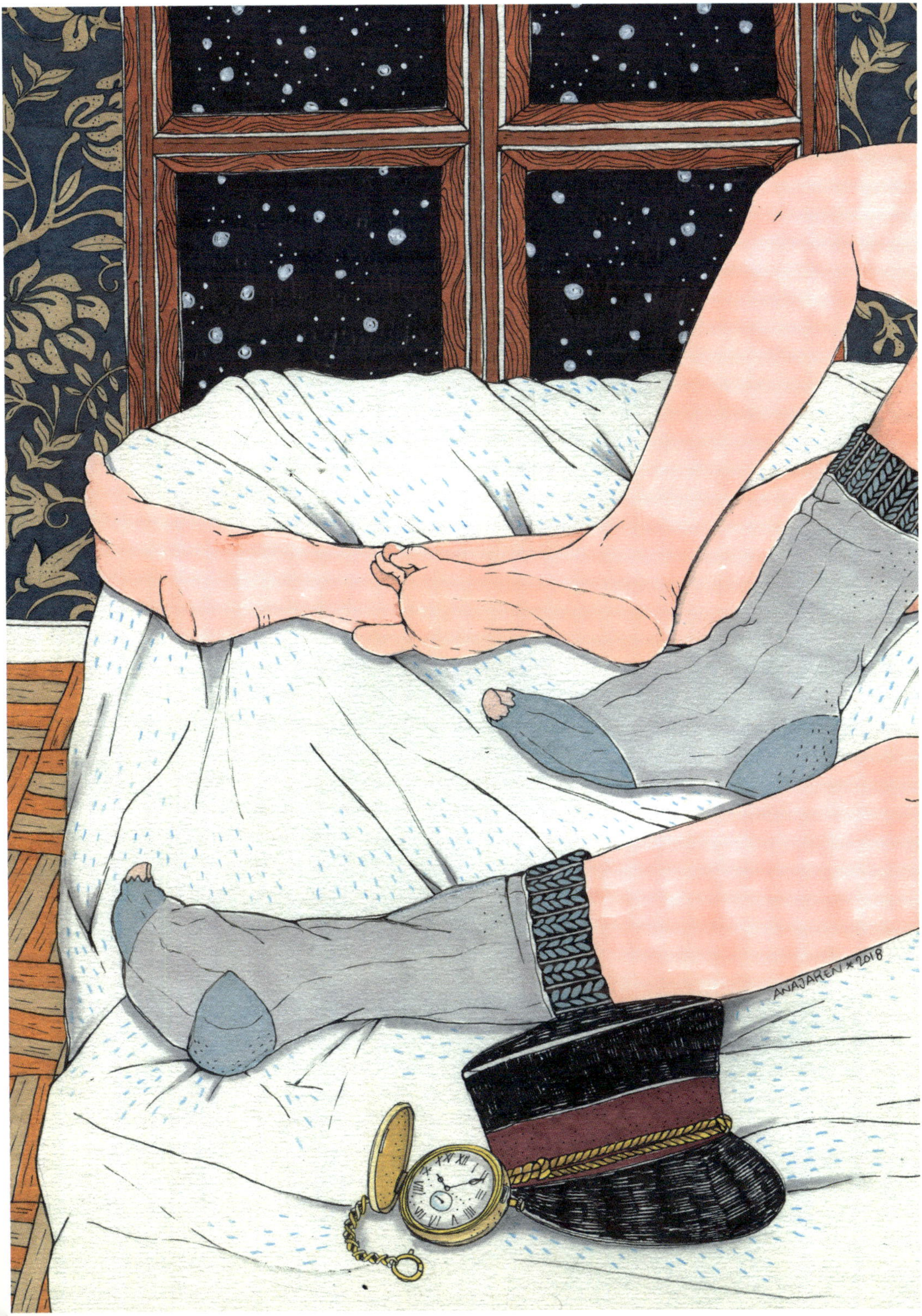
ANAJAREN × 2018

WOLF

Nathan Jones

With me is a dying wolf.
It took thirty men stinking of fish to haul him back
The knot forming
A kind of net, except those that were trapped
Were the ones he closed like a fist around him.

50 days nothing coming or to come for
The doctor's boy sang outside in the corridor about
Gills still ticking, those who had been
Monstrously gutted.

He told me to shut myself up
As if his tongue itself was sharp enough
To carve a hole for food in my face
His glare projecting the suspect into my chest
His slack mouth around it the music of my life.

What is the desert
When every day the wolf and I entered into tiredness
Like it was a sea
Onto the surface of which our backs rose and fell.
The pearl cracked, veined, with fine blood
Capsizing him. The outside took us in.

LEOPARD

Yorùbá Hunter Poem

Gentle hunter
His tail plays on the ground
While he crushes the skull.

Beautiful death
Who puts on a spotted robe
When he goes to his victim.

Playful killer
whose loving embrace
Splits the antelope's heart.

SLUG

Johnny Whitney

My visitor tonight,
let's just call him Mr. Slug
because he doesn't want to tell me his real name
also
because he is the fattest motherfucker
in the known history of fat motherfuckers

The floor manager
At some discount furniture store
literally renting used couches
to broke single moms
can you imagine it?

He doesn't want
to take his shirt off
He's over 300 pounds
that's probably for the best.

I reach to unbuckle his belt.
He's tells me he's taking a music appreciation night class
and is trying to "get" Debussy
and would I be interested in a classical music mixtape?

I attempt to unbutton his jeans.
He tells me favorite book is
"How to make friends and influence people" by Dale Carnegie
His mentor gave it to him in college
and it's been very helpful in his career.

I grab him by his cheeks,
pull his enormous face in for a fat red kiss.
His mother's name is Carol.
His mother's dog's name is Caroline.
His favorite song is Neil Diamond's Sweet Caroline.

I know all this
because this fat piece of shit
has not stopped talking for the last 20 minutes

I grip the elastic of his underwear
His voice gets tiny
He breaks eye contact

He wonders
if maybe
he can call me “Jin”?

There’s this girl at work
in sales
Her name is “Jin”
1st generation Chinese immigrant
so beautiful
slender
pale
perfect.

He gave her a ride home once
seemed like they made a real connection
but upon leaving
he was too chickenshit to move in for a kiss.

Even if he were a millionaire she’d never want him.

He’s brought a picture of her from some corporate event
If I could maybe pull my hair up like her?
He’s also brought in a very slutty looking kimono,
would I mind changing into it real quick?
“um...Jin”?

I close the bathroom door.

Somewhere beyond this roof
a hot air balloon
will collide with a flock of migrating birds
and spring a flock of holes
and become the opposite of a balloon
and the opposite of a birthday present.

And somewhere else beyond this roof
A baby will be born
deaf
it will never hear the shittiest music ever written
Christian Rap, the clarinet, Jazz fusion or Silverchair

And somewhere even farther beyond this roof
My mother is staring at a child
from the window of a moving bus
Judging.

I slip into the kimono
trying to imagine how it feels to live for 30 years
as the 300 pound punchline to a joke
To be unwanted
Eternally
To be disqualified from authentic love
Forever.

But I cannot manage to conjure up any pity
I am haunted
By the curdling horror of my visitors
cock
A tiny nightmare
Pale as an undressed almond
A monument
to all things frail and undesired.

GOLEM

Fiona Pitt-Kethley

In my room is Golem.

He is unlike all the others.
No way to make him come.
Like a machine.
He has a half-formed look, almost a man,
gray as clay, unfinished and unfinishing,
more than a man simply in terms of strength.
A creature made by magic
in an attic.

The name of God slotted beneath his tongue,
rampaging out of his Master's control.
He'll be the end of me
unless I can unmake him.
Take the word away from him
and turn his matter
back to simple dust.

MONEY

Jenny Rossander

My visitor is Money

Tinkle tinkle on the stairs
Bodes extravagant intro

A single gold coin falls through
the keyhole
Then

Bang! He jumps in
With 40ties swing music tempo

Winks to me under his
Sharply trimmed brows
And turns my ceiling lamp
into a chandelier

He kisses my cat fondly
into a panther with a diamond leash
Zapps my wardrobe
Into Haute Couture
Dances around
pointing this way and that
Grinning his triangle dollar grin

Until my room resembles a
Parisian luxury suite
My cereal has turned into
Cocaine
And my breasts
are 3 sizes bigger

Finally he stands with wild
ecstatic eyes
In the center of his creations

Loud and slow
Like citing some ancient ritual
I let fall the last piece of underwear
And bow my head

'Behold Money, I am Woman.'

EAR/WINDOW

Nathan Jones

Still, he waits listening to the thrum of my stomach
Like a hall in which voiceless people rolled over the wooden floor
Every so often opening up to engulf one into its garden

Wreathing, before dropping some way to the thick river
Which spread them through the marshland
Where they lay dazzled in the clicking water, with the city

The city's aggregate undertone of creaking seams. He loves
Telling me about that strata of horizons. Eye teeming by my belly button.
My bare taught flesh a diffusion screen his plasma's dreams

Were thrown up on. The tambourine
Hardens sweating with his face. Suspicious like a boy listening
To his parents rattling the cups downstairs. Waxwork doll

Sliding over. And – and nothing – savouring silence
Because when I slept, his siege began. Eyes blank as
A father's trophy cabinet rationed by the darkness

Worrying dirt through the skin's pink pores.
Flamboyant underneath, a teenage boy is like an old man
Who has been turned inside out. The blackness

They see everything through some web of moon's hair.
When he pissed into the bucket in the corner of the room
It flowed so freely I breathed out. Opened the window:
Promise come back.

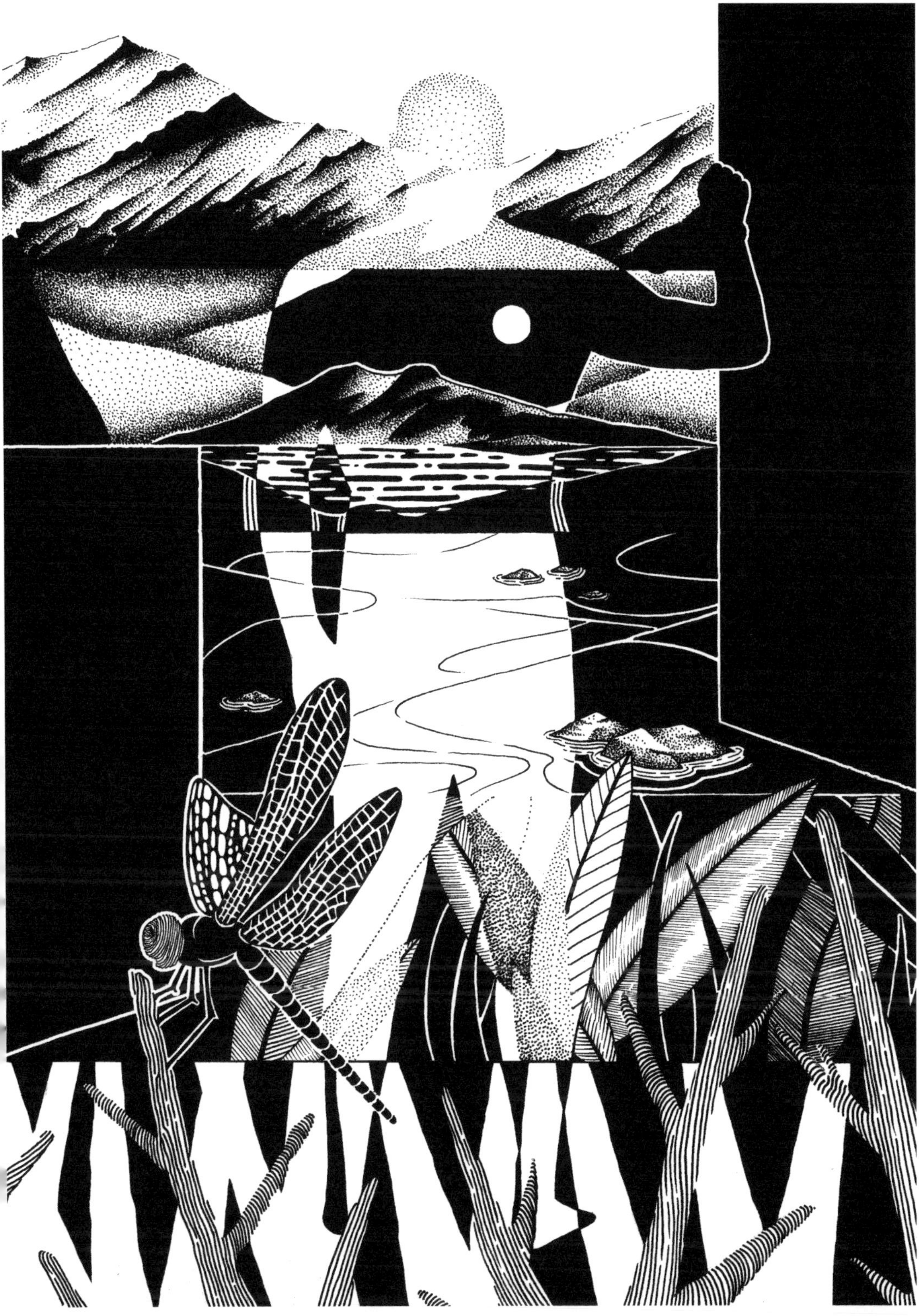

HYENA MAN

Yorùbá Hunter Poem

The scruffy one
Who eats the meat
Together with the bag
In which it is kept.
The greedy one,
Who eats the mother
And does not spare the child
God's bandy-legged creature.
Killer in the night.

2018. Oct

CORMORANT

Fiona Pitt-Kethley

My visitor is a cormorant

His scraggy neck makes me believe he's thin
until I see the rest, in dusty black.
He hangs his oily mac up by the door,
spread out to dry across a couple of hooks.

Eyes close together, face a little sharp,
intent on getting everything he wants.
He loves my fishy smell and dives right in

TRAFFIC JAM

Jenny Rossander

My visitor is a Traffic Jam

'Just do something' He says
'Anything'

So I curl back and back
Until I'm moon shaped
Let loose a soft humming sound
Wrap a leg around his neck
While
NO! Not That!

We stop. It's fine. It happens.
I gather my strength again
Look him deeply in the eyes
Roll my hip ever so slowly
Left hand on his chest
Right hand in his memory
Of warm summer teenage flings
With every saturated colour
That comes with those
Thumb tickling the dull flame
That rests between the recollections
I can't help but smile as I
Feel myself becoming her
Little Camilla with the blond
Braids
No Please! Not there!

I clench my fist to not shout
At him.
Deep breath now

For a while we're in complete
Gridlock
And every car stands unmoving
And the tension is
Unbearable

Ok.
Again
Something else

With all my self-control
We start over

This time I'm a laughing bulldozer
Pushing him into the mattress
Dirty jokes in his ear
Grip him with a firm hand
Don't give him a moment to speak
I scream like mental as he enters

Like I've never experienced a half-flacci…

No! I can't! I'm sorry!

Deep
Breath
Now…

I'm surrounded by red light
By stop signs
By angry drivers
In angry cars

I give him a moment

Close my eyes and
sort my shopping list
In my head

Coffee, bread, lube, shampoo

Ignoring the honking sounds
Of him panicking

They die down quickly
Anyway

The door slams so hard

A pinching whiplash
On my pride.

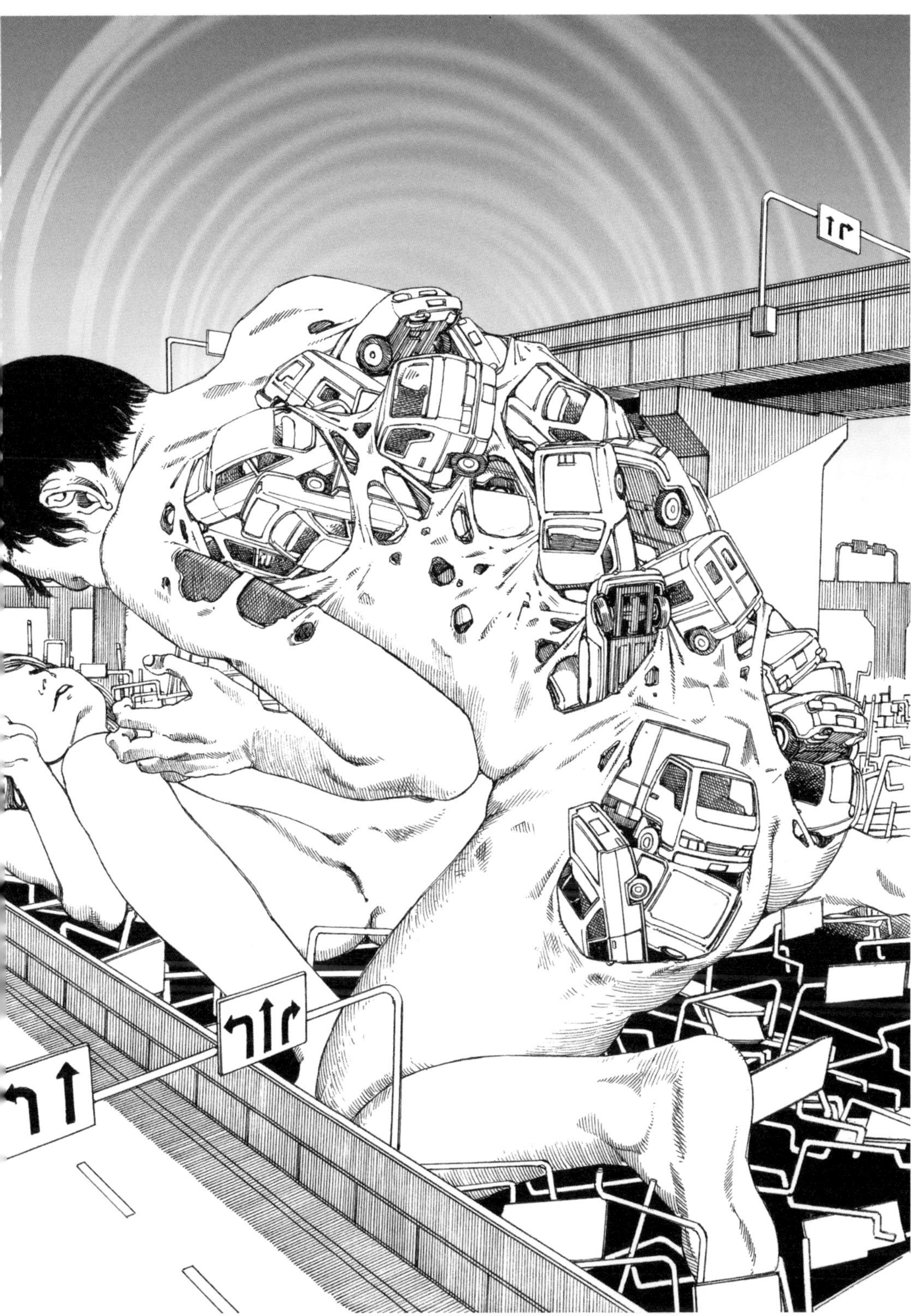

HORSE

Timothy Bruzon

My visitor is a horse
Unpredictable
Prone to biting

Lick!

He feeds from my palm
Fumbling around for sugar lumps
Unnerving me with his clumsiness

Snip!

Yellow teeth snap together like magnets
Too close to the open fingers of my wet hand

Clack!

He drops to all fours
Keen to feel my skin on his back
I lean in close, my breasts on his shoulder
Calmly whispering into his ear
I stroke his nose, praising his leggy elegance
And stare deep into his willing obsidian eyes

CRACK!

With me he can exist in the ignorant bliss of his horseness
Never wondering whether he could have run faster or jumped higher,
Never inspired to dance by the rhythm of his hooves
He always accepts the whip, unflinching and compliant
Happy to be ridden whether he wants it or not.

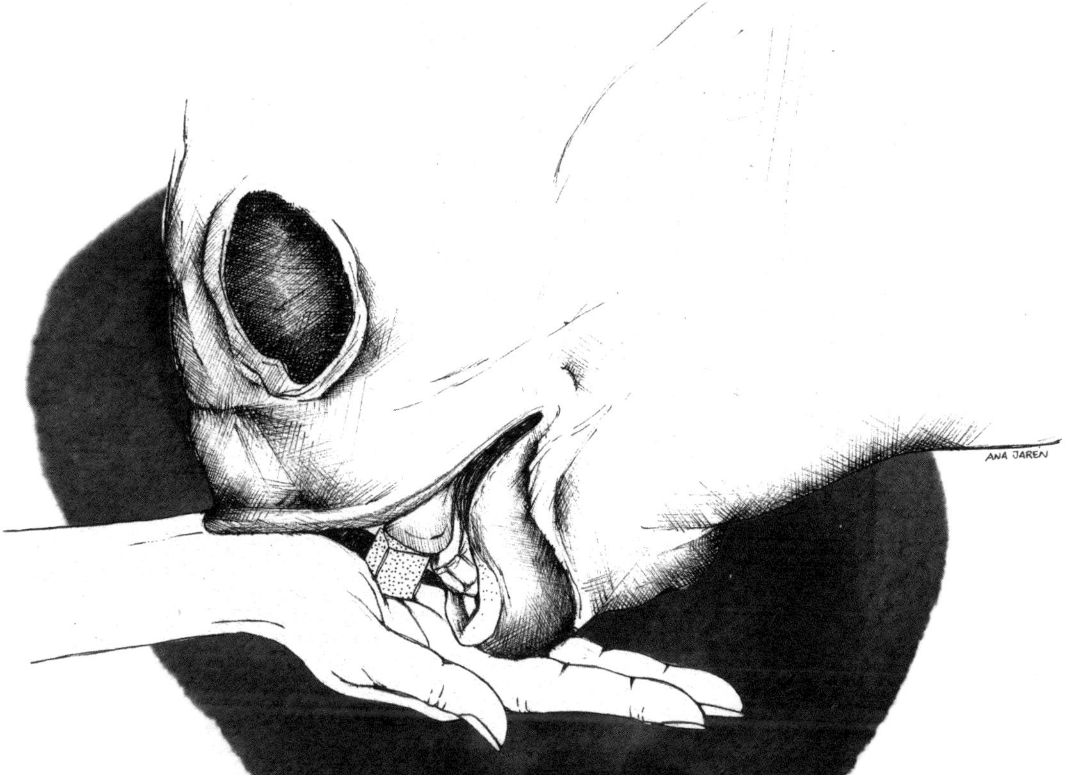
ANA JAREN

FISH

Nathan Jones

The kind of man you believe in, rather than be with.
Believed in bed. Bead with.
But you can't gaze at a shadow ploughing dim lights
part of a song you wouldn't notice if someone wasn't playing
it wrong, this uncle without portfolio
the fish

come like a Bluetooth signal with flickering relation to the
device, bodies:
the wilting one I offer up under the sibilant moon or the white
sun for snubbing away with thumbs. A special function to find
within these dark signals the difference this man's voice
makes in the world his hands roam
free through.

The room, his whisper the quick strokes
of scissors sibilant in its own jaws behind both my ears:
I have nothing. I have not much. I have enough. I have everything,
What with what with what? With what with what? What wish with?

A flame set inside my mind with no oxygen to feed it.
Philosophies are
conspiratorial and reconnoiteritive when they are this quiet.
Having no sense of short-circuiting the flesh they crawl across,
or through. Mouth snatching the air before:
Not something I am used to, in this age of information,

the equilibrium it brings when a voice is applied directly:
its sword in a moment of coldness interior to execution,
cleaves my throat,
he's saying.

THE EGÚNGÚN

Tade Ipadeola

With me tonight is a masked man
he-who-must-not-be-named
who covers himself with mirrors
and the smell of distant planets.

He growls for speech and grunts
continually his carnal ecstasies.
His body is old and lean and full
of experience and the night.

He sheds every apparel on him
except the mask, except the carved
mask with a dozen ivory heads
of which an uncle once told
a strange story high on pot.

My guest makes me wonder within
if they teach arithmetic
in the world beyond my own-
he pays exactly what I ask
and not a naira more.

He is albino, has a tattoo
of a clock on his smooth belly:
twelve sharp,
midday or midnight I don't know

He offers his clay pipe in the time
he has left on the clock
but I must decline
as politely as I can.

TREE

Aaron Perrino

With me is a tree
blowing in the wind
Wherever I go
its leaves caress my skin
Branches break
as timber shakes my core
A forest of senses
Falling to the floor.

I admire
This giant beauty of ancient oak
Lying restful
in a cloud of cigarette smoke
Handsome spirit in a garden adored.
A chorus of caws, growls,
and howls

A jungle expansive
ready to be explored.

ANAJARÉN

ME

Hendrik Willemyns

My visitor is me.
Or who I might have been
If I hadn't dated Oscar Didriksen
in second grade.

She comes to me in dreams.
A quantum technician from Berkeley
Still smoking like California in the eighties.
Before it was outlawed.

We cuddle and tell each other
how much we envy ourselves
And when we are done smiling
we sing our song together

like planets sending spaceships to each other

We are an astronaut drifting in space
lost between numbers
impossible to see
forever alone.

ANA JARÉN

ANTELOPE

Yorùbá Hunter Poem

A creature to pet and spoil
Like a child.
Smooth skinned
Stepping cautiously
In the lemongrass
Round and plump
Like a newly married wife.
The neck
Heavy with brass rings.
The eyes
Gentle like a bird's.
The head
Beautiful like carved wood.
When you suddenly escape
You spread fine dust
Like a butterfly
Shaking its wings.
Your neck seems long,
So very long
To the greedy hunter.

Creature of
HIROYUKI Y.
H. Yamada
2018. Oct.

SHEEP

Jenny Rossander

With me is a big furry sheep

People get lost in his white curls
Candy floss textured
That has grown so big around him
That's it's hard to see his real shape
He tells me he is strong and muscular within
To carry the weight of all that wool

He likes it when I fall asleep in him
And he almost can't see me
Or the room
Or anything
He will stay like that for days
Covering my bed like whipped cream
Dazed by his own outfit
And I get the best sleep on him
In a land of white hairs

Doesn't even notice the times I invite
other guest to lounge in his wooly landscape

Soft and shiftable
He comes to me
To have me command him

As predictable men goes
He could be their grandmaster
Excelling generic submissiveness into an art form
Gripping me ever so softly
When he comes
then always apologises
Through the sound of my laughter

Some days I ask him to stand by the window
while I drink my tea
So the sunlight shines through him
Revealing the trembling silhouette
of a little lamb

LOUSE

Johnny Whitney

My visitor tonight
is a louse
scourged
reviled
crawling scalps
in hiding beneath hairs as tall as skyscrapers

I picked him up
at some shit for brains sports bar
tequila shots at 11:30 in the afternoon
his eyes the opposite
of neon

Droning on and on
wouldn't I for just one moment
consider the horror of life
as a louse?

Erupted at birth
ripped from from a bleach cold egg
Marooned
an infant wandering an alien sphere

Within a day
you meet a brother, a sister, another brother another
all like you
weeping uncontrollably
bellies boiling with hunger

A rumor starts
that your food is literally
the ground that you are walking on
The joy is beyond words
the feast is explosive

Within seconds your children
are in the thousands
a civilization

In the motel
he paces as I undress
Barely interested in my flesh
a tentative king

Any day now without warning they will find him

The sky's gaping maw
will vomit a sheet of chemicals
those that are not seared
into death
will wake to a ground sown with poison

I crawl
into bed
between starched motel sheets
and wait
for him to just fucking die already

MOTEL

THE WRITER

Leen Diependaele

My visitor tonight
Can't stop thinking about
Writing a hidden novel with me

One only I should read
Dedicated lines
In which he can be free

He starts straight away
Samples new words for
Nature's surrounding
Addictive desire
Fulfilling touch
Seizing the present

My visitor tonight is nervous
He never thought
He would come here
And ask for

But his vocabulary
Contains only vowels
I'm sure they mean more
Than I can conceive

I react on his anthem
Alternate
Short shouts
With long breaths

Characters we are
But not together
Writing his novel

24H STARBUCKS™

Jenny Rossander

I am a 24 Hour open hectic Starbucks™

...I guess word got around
People on their way to work
People needing time to think
People with nothing but time
People on the floor, on chairs,
In the windows, on the roof,

I pour myself into assorted
Positions
In different size paper cups
Some like me hot and sizzling
Crawling on the floor making cat sounds
For others I'm a frozen
Ice blend
Reluctantly unzipping

They place orders at my front desk
'One shot decaff americano - no Milk!!'
'One double tongue latex french - No eyecontact!'

My menu is long and diverse
Sometimes a newcomer
Confused by the menu
Not knowing the game
Will take my hand
And ask for
'Just coffee, please'

BUFFALO

Yorùbá Hunter Poem

The buffalo is the death
That makes a child climb a thorn tree.
When the buffalo dies in the forest
The head of the household hides in the roof.
When the hunter meets the buffalo
He promises never to hunt again.
He will cry out: 'I only borrowed the gun!
I only look after it for my friend!'
Little he cares about your hunting medicines:
He carries two knives on his head,
Little he cares about your Dane gun,
He wears the thickest skin.
He is the butterfly of the savannah:
He flies along without touching the grass.
When you hear thunder without rain
It is the buffalo approaching.

All Things
Ballad Of Sir
(Let It Roll)
I'd Have You A
Isn't It A Pity
Just For Today
The Light

BROWN BEAR

Jenny Rossander

My visitor is a big brown bear

He roars my name fondly
As he tumbles over the doorstep
Like we're already old friends
On a chance encounter in
A foreign land

He wants nothing specific
Just touch me like you do
Old gal!

Paws at a tit with booming
Laughter
Tickles my thigh with his beard
Tells me stories while I go
Exploring in his big brown coat

He has had 30 different
Boring jobs
Which add up to a quite
Curious tale
When put together

He has had 100 different
Exciting women
Which is equally engaging
So while he talks of Clarice,
Vanessa, Mary and so on
My explorations take me deeper
Into his gigantic form

Swim in an armpit
Dive into a dark pocket
Slide down a spine
Lick at a claw
Smell the winter cave he
Slumbered in
Taste the sour taste of
Endless pine forests
Nibble at a cone

I climb to his shoulder
And whisper in his ear

All the wonders I found in him

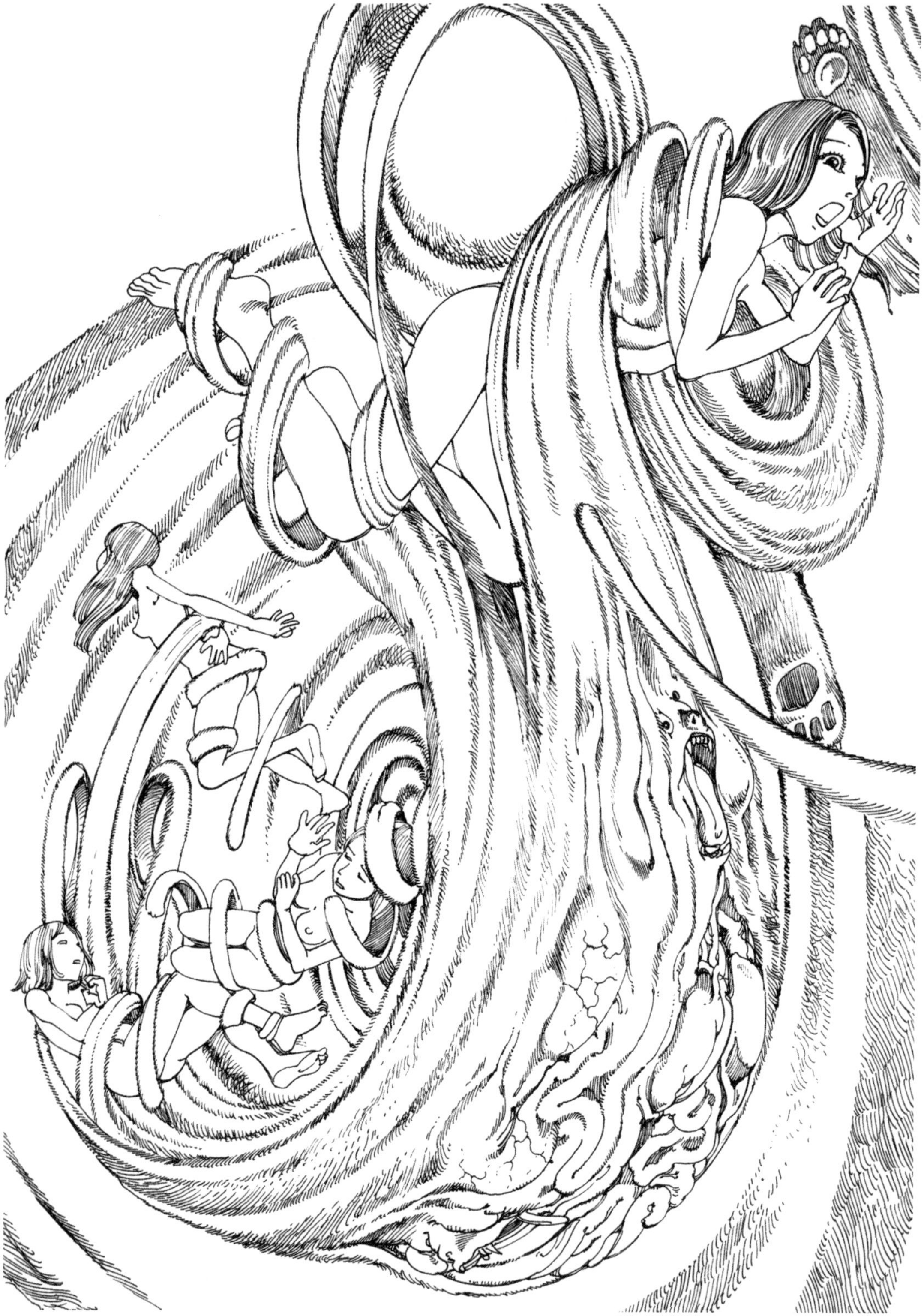

PERFECT

Johnny Whitney

My visitor tonight is perfect

His eyes
brilliant as the hot light
from a mountain of priceless 18th century rococo paintings
set on fire.
My skin is as cold as an empty phone booth
so I come to him.

His walk
brazen as a diving falcon
who's rushing rooms cannot conceive the concept of walls.
In the dark underwear hotel,
I long of him.

His sweat
I drink it by the jug in broad daylight
I never feel ashamed.
He says my lips are thrilling as a jungle cat.
But I know
my tongue is a frail, deaf diamond.
So I thirst for him.

His mattress
forever melted to the basement of my mind.
I swear its a portal to some unauthorized heaven.
My homes are junkyards filled with pine scented air fresheners
so I stalk him, I hunt for him.

His pupils
could easily be confused
for civilization scrambling black holes.
The end.

Whiskey drunk
I stumble down to the canals,
wade hip deep into the water
and wait for his ship to come in amongst damp hallucinations

His gaze
like streetlights reflected in the street after long rain
haunts me.
I'll catch a ray of him if I can
bottle it tight like a firefly in a jar.

Because tonight he is with me
teeth to teeth
belly to belly
breath to breath
but tomorrow he'll be gone
a vapor
a phantom
and I'll be here
wishing everything weren't so goddam un-effervescent.

ORANGES

Chika Unigwe

With me tonight
Is the smell of oranges
Of lavender
Of a partner (a wife?) left behind

He calls me Julie or honey or sweet thing
Tells me to bite his ears
Suck his nipples
Hold his cock

He tastes of sweat
And guilt and dreams
He calls me his Nubian princess
And when he comes

He moans a name
That ricochets around the room
Bouncing off walls
A name

That is not mine
Which drags him back
Pulls him off me
And leads him out

Back home (?)

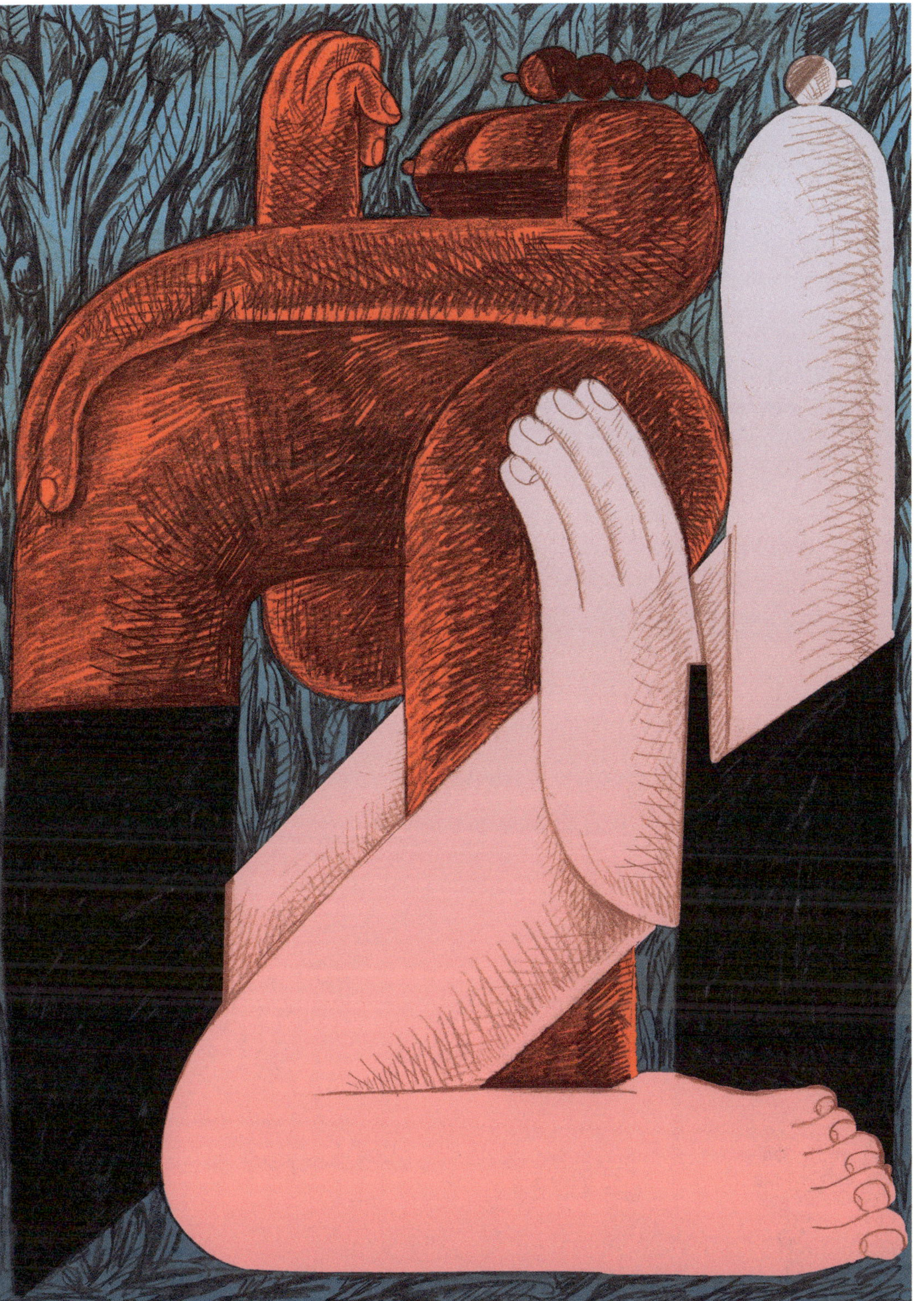

MOON

Aaron perrino

With me is a moon
shining on a meaningless world
an infinite joy
from which spring is born

It nurses my darkness back to life
from a cold winter gaze
to summer light

ANAJARÉN * LABARIBARUSKA 2016

SNOW GLOBE

Jenny Rossander

With me is a Snow Globe

When I shake him
He lights up the entire room

With glitter and white specs

And we swim in it

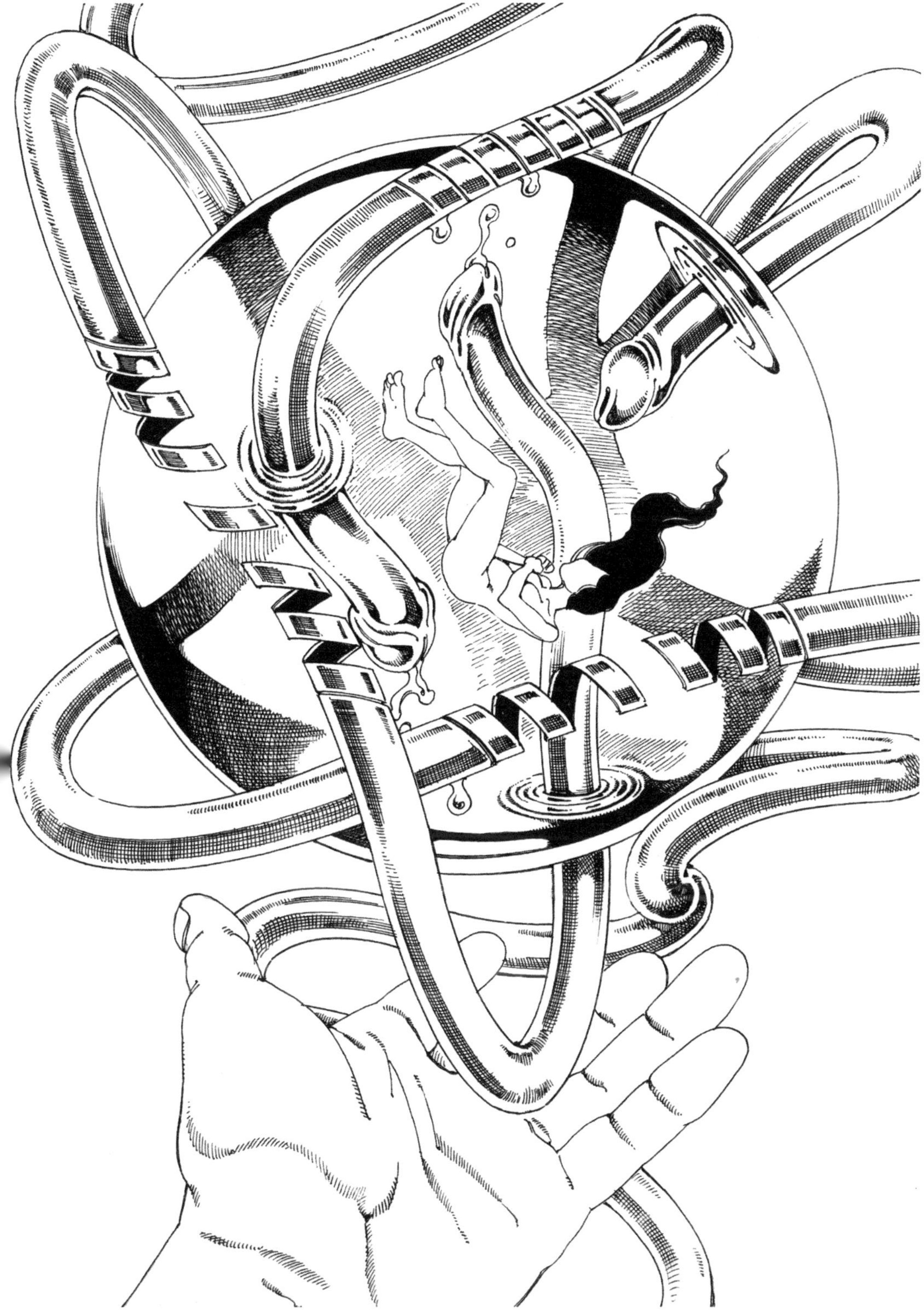

DODO

Fiona Pitt-Kethley

My visitor is a Dodo

He pauses for a moment at my door
and enters slowly, ponderously.
He has a mark left by his spectacles
around his bleary eyes. He's read too much.
He seems the last of an extinct species,
bred in the dusty air of libraries,
ungainly, slightly fat. He'll never fly.

He leaves his motley plumage neatly-draped
across the back of a chair by the bed.
The folds and wrinkles of his flesh seem like
another set of clothes above claw feet.
With a fussy flapping of wings and squawks
he beats his pigeon chest. It is over now.

DEAD MAN

Timothy Bruzon

My visitor is a dead man
Or what's left of one
The muscle and fat stripped
In the years since his passing.

With my arms around him
I can see the palm of my hand
When we kiss my breath
slips between his bones.

His pelvis scrapes my flesh
His elbows hammer and crack
And yet he's warm to the touch
Sensitive as teeth.

Sometimes he pulls himself apart
A puzzle that upsets itself
And I slowly
piece him back together.

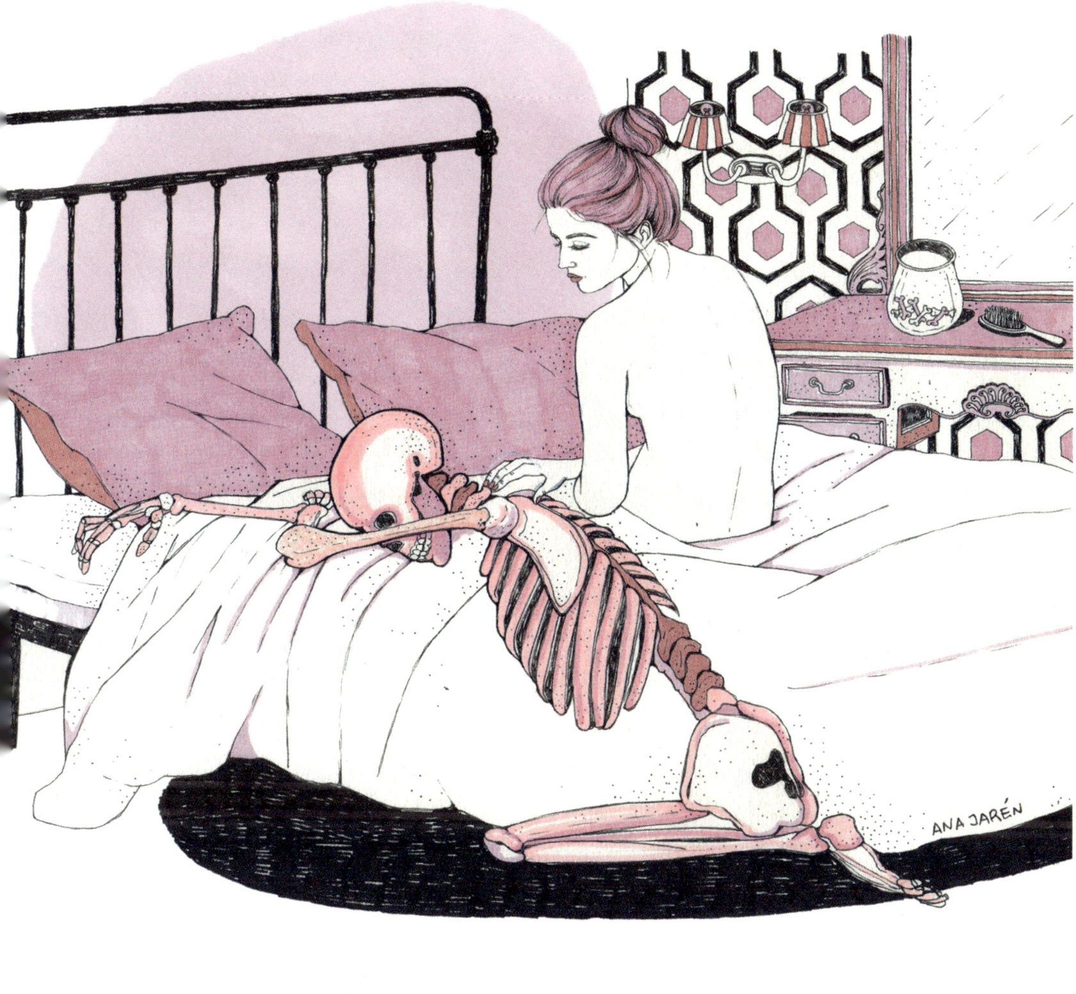
ANA JARÉN

ALL THE VACANT FIELDS OF CHINA

Jenny Rossander

All the vacant fields of China

Such is the sadness in his
Greying eyes

'I knew you when you
were just a little child,'

'I've known you since
Phanerozoic times.'

Joke unappreciated

I see a building block
demolish in his left pupil
As he raises an eyebrow
at me.

I wonder if he's here
because he knew me
Or in spite of it

As he wipes saliva off his chin
with a sleeve
A river pollutes in his nostrils

I help him out of his pants
He plays with my breast
like a small child

I help him in
He knows it from there

In his veins high speed trains
Ride over old retired tracks
His vocal chords can't carry
The scream that builds in him
And he collapses like a
rusting car in a junk yard
Finally giving in to its own weight

I roll my eyes
And call for an ambulance

MECHANIC

Nathan Jones

The blindness of a mechanic
entering the silk after a day in oil
distorting a body with his hands, plunging into it,
while he attends to a separation of activity
from spirit. He is careful only of his own brevity –
nothing else turns so quickly from the new
into the drawn out.

The organic quickness he works with,
a nest of rhythms that made this world, is terrifying:
if someone were to explore my body with this speed
I thought, it would not be long before I am found.

But not a body – it is steel
whose will has been distorted in the heat,
that has ceased to become merely a surface
and grows deep in its own heart.

A quick distance that assembles,
the door where boys stand,
a slow closeness that takes apart
while the white light shakes on the black table.

His was a simple existence

such a long way from anything:
if someone were to reinvent our cities with this sureness,
I think, the fumes that have destroyed them might vanish
back into their burrow, calming. Like a cigarette.
In our togetherness we lost that slow purpose.
Repaired it with urgency.

Everything that became so slowly old, become sudden
as the end always is. Careless man –
the stroke of the engine absent
from the feeling that propels the heavy
clockwork head, descending.

SPIKE

Johnny Whitney

My visitor tonight
Is an un-rusted railroad spike
Sharp as a broken gin bottle
Harder than prison bars

I have been cast to play the part
of the perpetual shattering machine
the delicate belle
soft, pulsating organs
The tongue with no bones
heart unsheathed
by its wide, flat nail

My instructions are
to await him like an advancing army

So I've spent the last 48 hours
marinating in a broth
of air conditioning and bad motel art
perfecting my impression
of a poorly painted tiger lily

A prearranged knock
The un-rusted railroad spike at the door
A short, small creature
perhaps the height of a 13 year old boy
beady eyes
shuttered
all tenderness evicted

seems like the kind of asshole
that sprints around the office to business meetings
just to get a jog in

He asks me what the fuck
I'm waiting for?
complains that he
asked for a girl with bigger tits
and specifically asked for me
to be wearing Yves Saint Laurent Rouge Volupte Perle Lipstick
shade #108 Celestial Mauve
and for fuck sake
No high heels.

In the bedroom
I crystalize
and shatter for him again
and again
and again
He thinks he fucks like a factory programmed to ruin
like a bulldozer excavating a boneyard
He demands I enumerate
His many similarities to a wrecking ball

Yet
the transaction is mercifully quick
5 minutes…
maybe
more

And afterwards
In the dark
All is calm
I remain un-devastated
The curtains sigh

His face
a blanket of flesh
beneath which
I hear teeth grinding
As loud as traffic

I nearly laugh
he reminds me
of a pile of ash
in an ashtray
Frantically trying to mold itself back into a fresh new cigarette

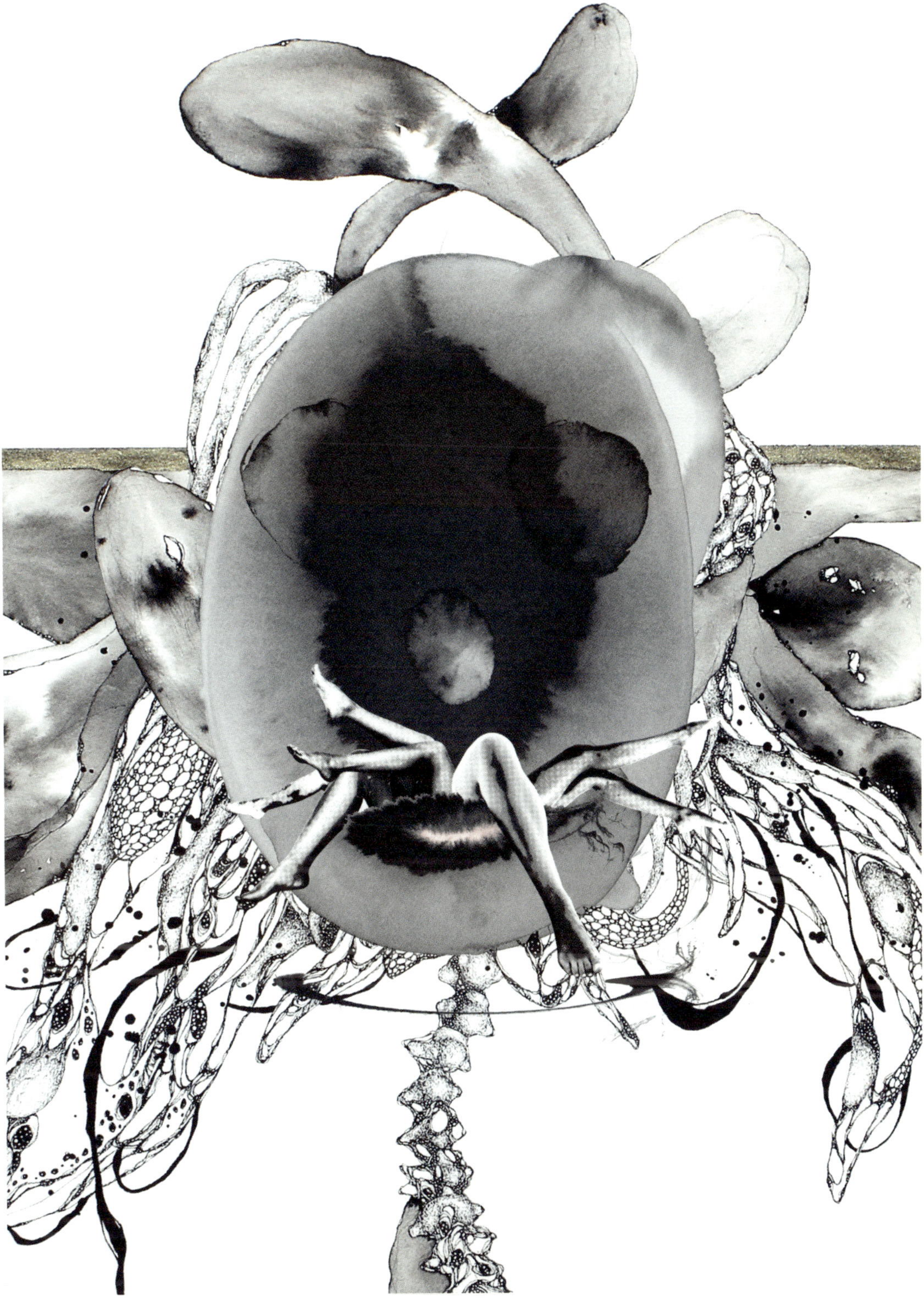

CLOUD/PUDDLE

Jenny Rossander

My visitor is a cloud
when he comes in
Breezing through the gap over my door

Trembles for a moment
And then rains himself everywhere
In such a dear tantrum
Until there is no more cloud left
Just a puddle on the floor
That screams "come here!"

I sit down and look into the surface
He is all transparent there
Apologetically looking up at me
Under that
Dreams of guitars
Past girlfriends
College degrees
And even early memories

He moans shyly at the exposure
So with my hands
Very carefully
I scrape him over the floors
Little wave after wave
Until we are both hiding under my table
Like kids at a party

A place to tell secrets
Sift through the past
The saddest childhood
Rock band ambitions
And a hole where
sunny family gardens should be.

Delicate plants spring
from my wooden floorboards
And he grows warmer
Imaginary paintings ripple in his surface
As I put my chin into it
Drops of him cling to my eyelashes
And I cry a few of his tears for him

DRAGON

Fiona Pitt-Kethley

With me is a dragon

Small eyes are fixed on mine. His reptile gaze
takes in my room, my body on the bed…
He's into Wagner and likes leather too.
Wears very little else. His trousers creak.
His walk is ponderous, regally slow.
His long coat trails behind him like a tail.
He's tight with money, guards his treasure well,
too cautious to shed clothes with others round.
Dear God, his breath, whenever he comes close,
so strong, that you could light it with a match.

DRILL MONKEY

Yorùbá Hunter Poem

We invite her to die
She smiles.
She dies at last
Her cheeks full of laughter
Two rows of bared white teeth.

At daybreak
The housewife sweeps the floor
The eagle sweeps the sky
And Drill Monkey
Sweeps the top of her tree.

Abuse her
And she will follow you home.
Praise her
And she leaves you alone.
The ragged man
And the man in the embroidered gown
Both covet her skin.

Lice killer
With black nails
Deep-set eyes
Sweeping tail.
Too beautiful to live.
Death always follow greed.
Too beautiful to survive
Death always follow war.

2018. Oct.

THE PRIEST

Timothy Bruzon

My visitor is a priest
Middle aged and beautiful
The voice of God loud and real in his ear

At his request I unhinge my mind
From any lingering notions of faith
The last thing he wants is deference
Just soft buttocks and swinging tits.

Each part of the body has its own divinity
Each zone its devoted worshippers

He gives thanks for the sweat in my armpits
The heat of my inner thigh
Our shuddering deep breath
And the grip of my fingers

At that moment
He can see all things in all time
A beginning, a middle and an end
Slammed together in one unending image

I don't even get close.

ANA JARÉN

BLACK ASTRONAUT

Jenny Rossander

With me is you, Black Astronaut

You're so sedated
I hardly recognize

You used to be the prism in my window
Throwing rainbows at my walls
And all those stories
Of galaxies, stars and supernovas
That we would unwrap between my sheets

You would come to me
Always when I least expected it
Bringing music divine
In a hurricane of excitement

Travel dust drizzling from your boots

Dragging my laughing hands to the window
To point out things in the sky

"Oh you can't even imagine it!"
You said
With thunder in your eyes

So gloomy to see you now
A shadow hiding deep in my pillows
At certain intervals
Sighing
the darkest breaths

I wonder
Did you stray too far on your astral journeys?
What did you find?

WHITE SOCKS

Chika Unigwe

I had an aunt whose husband wore white socks only too.
I tell him this.
He looks at me as if surprised to hear me talk

I am a horse in a circus. A lion. A tiger
Tamed and forced to perform
Jumping through hoops

Pirouetting.
But there are times, like tonight
I forget and escape my role

I wear colored socks too. Not just today.
He tells me this.
He looks at me as if I were someone else

He dips the bed when he sits on it.
I have broken the spell. Ruined the night.
Circus acts do not speak

He has his head in his hands.
Thin blond hair like corn silk
Spill over his hands

I have a father who loves corn.
I do not tell him this.
Boiled. Roasted. Covered in soot

My father would eat it
I see my father now only in dreams
Gagged. Limping. Not a corn in sight

Blond hair lifts his head.
His trousers are back on
His shirt is still unbuttoned

He will be getting up soon
I fear
Calculating my loss

You will have to pay…something.
I tell him this.
No pro bono in my line of work

He peels off a note.
Then another. Then another.
Points at my blouse

I begin to take it off
The world is righted
The circus is back in town

FULL MOON

Tsu Ye - 3rd Century Geisha Poet

I cannot sleep for the blaze of the full moon.
I thought I heard here and there
a voice calling,
hopelessly I answer “Yes” to the empty air.

It is night again.
I let down my silken hair over my shoulders and open my
thighs over my lover.
‘Tell me, is there any part of me that is not lovable?’

I had not fastened my sash over my gown
when you asked me to look out the window.
If my skirt fluttered open, blame the spring wind.

The bare branches tremble in the sudden breeze.
The twilight deepens.
My lover loves me, and I am proud of my young beauty.

I am the North Pole steady for a thousand years.
Your sun-like heart goes east in the morning and west in the evening.

INUIT

Grant Hart

His skin was like creamy alabaster
polished to a smooth gloss or white jade.
More like the jade because he was jaded as Hell.

He looked Asian, so much so that he advertised himself as an
Asian exotic dancer and he really got into his work,
especially when Japanese men would stuff twenty dollar bills
into his speedos and said things like "you are the most
beautiful Japanese man I ever saw... only a Japanese man can
be so beautiful!" Or "Only Korean men are as beautiful as you"
or "What part of China do you come from?"

The fact is he was not Asian at all. He was Inuit, an Eskimo
and his skin was not like jade but like ice.

EXIT

Mike Ladd

One day
before I launch from this room
straight through the roof
I will count all the dry specks of flesh
my men have left

there must be dunes meters high
if I cupped them in my hand
blew them to the sky
they would join stars
constellations of memories,
ambitions, tiny drifters on lightyears

dandruff, the dust of angst
floats in my client's half sweet tear
when I take off from my catapult chair
the flecks of skin will bluster
like rocket ship smoke
and I'll be gone.

TEN YEARS & THREE DAYS

An Qi

Who will be my guest today?
A plane, sunshine, plants or confusion?

Plane brushes over the blue sky like a roaring mop
Sweeping distance and dust before landing safe

Sunshine seems perfect these days, rare for Beijing also
Shining brightly like a highland you are among the rarest

Plants consume me on my windowsill, consume my breath
My gaze, sorrow and joy while remaining quiet

They never say anything
But keep sprouting
Loving the world with events
Or incidents happening daily as I do

Ah confusion
Clock, removed of second and minute hand
Stays still, the best way to defend against death

I pretend that time exists not
Like you—

It's ten years & three days since
You left me

QUIET TWIN BED

Olajumoke Verissimo

My visitor tonight is a quiet twin bed
Carrying pillows that have known sweat,
Fears and anxieties of men who turn amoeba
As I twist their body into a narrative of desires

My body a lonesome partner, confides
My wish for an audience on the bed—a stadia
Where thighs yield to sports of a hunger
Of love, that turn innards into singers

This bed has witnessed erosions before
Bed sheets stream down to a side as
Marathons of fantasies and dreams
Become ambitions fleshing into twined legs

On this bed were matches between nations
A white skin slapping a brown skin into bargain
Of animated moans finding convergence
In the rush of shaking shoulders and hope of bliss.

ILLUSTRATORS

Boris Pramatarov	10
Kensuke Saito	15
Shintaro Kago	17
Alice Morishita	19
Ana Jarén	21
Benjamin Hendlisz	23
Hiroyuki Yamada	25
Kensuke Saito	29
Shintaro Kago	33
Benjamin Hendlisz	35
Hiroyuki Yamada	37
Alice Morishita	39
Shintaro Kago	43
Ana Jarén	45
Benjamin Hendlisz	47
LRNZ	49
Ana Jarén	51
Ana Jarén	53
Hiroyuki Yamada	55
Shintaro Kago	58
Kensuke Saito	61
Tom Liekens	63
Shintaro Kago	65
Hiroyuki Yamada	67
Shintaro Kago	70
Boris Pramatarov	73
Eline Van Dam	75
Ana Jarén	77

Shinatro Kago	79
Alice Morishita	81
Ana Jarén	83
Shintaro Kago	86
Benjamin Hendlisz	89
Kensuke Saito	93
Shintaro Kago	96
Hiroyuki Yamada	99
Ana Jarén	101
Shintaro Kago	103
Eline Van Dam (2p)	105, 107
Riki Kadowaki	109
Studio-Takeuma	111
Owen Gent	113
Photo By Lisa Carletta (2p)	115, 116

Editor: *Hendrik Willemyns*
Publisher: *teshima*
Design: *Victor Robyn*
Cover image: *Ana Jarén*
Photo: *Rob Walbers*

www.teshima.be

distributed by Luster
www.lusterweb.com
info@lusterweb.com

ISBN: 9789460582479
NUR: 306, 660
D/2019/12.005/7

This book is also an album
The Original Soundtrack of Birdsong can be found on
www.teshima.be/soundtrack
Using this code: **2-33-5**

teshima